EVERYONE IS SOMEONE

About this book

This beautifully illustrated book is made of simple rhymes that teach children that we are all more similar than we are different—that everyone, everywhere, is someone.

Created by the company Sackcloth & Ashes, EVERYONE IS SOMEONE is an initiative to provide books and blankets to kids in foster care in the United States.

For each EVERYONE IS SOMEONE book purchased, a second book will be given to a child in foster care.

Our book may be purchased in bulk for wholesale, promotional, educational, or business use. For more information, please contact info@everyoneissomeone.com

Written by Bob Dalton | BobxDalton.com | @bobxdalton

Artwork by Ritchie Collins | RitchieCollinsGallery.co.uk | @ritchiecollins_

Printed in the United States

ISBN 978-0-578-72458-4

Dedication

To my Godson
Theonitus Walker Tardie:
As you grow up and get bigger and tall
some people will laugh when they see you fall
just get right up and brush right off
and always remember we need to love all.

EVERYONE IS SOMEONE

Written by **Bob Dalton** with artwork by **Ritchie Collins**

No matter how nice

no matter how mean

no matter how dirty

no matter how clean

no matter how rich

no matter how poor

no matter how l

no matter how more

no matter how cold

no matter how young

no matter how old

no matter how big

no matter how small

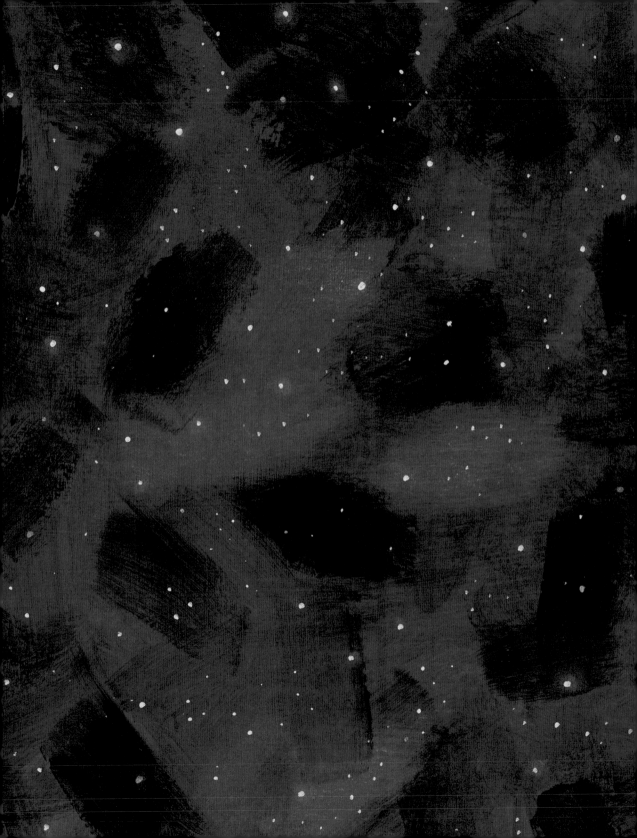

Biographies

BOB DALTON is the founder and CEO of Sackcloth & Ashes, a mission driven company that gives a blanket to a local homeless shelter for each one purchased. In 2018 he launched Blanket the United States, a campaign with the goal of donating one million blankets to homeless shelters by 2024. He now travels the United States campaigning to bring awareness and resources to organizations that are creating solutions for homelessness and speaking at events on the topics of entrepreneurship and societal solutions.

RITCHIE COLLINS was born on the west coast of Scotland and studied painting and illustration in Glasgow before settling in Edinburgh. His work is influenced by the Scottish coast and wild countryside. Celtic art, myths and Scottish folklore are a constant source of inspiration. Vibrant colour, simple form and a creative use of texture are woven together to give the original paintings their unique magical quality. Ritchie's paintings are created in mixed media using handmade papers, spray paints, oil pastel, acrylic, water mixable oil, acrylic inks and gold leaf. "All the things I paint come from dreams or memories of places I've been. What is important to me is trying to capture the true feelings of a place in time, rather than the reality." Each painting tells a story with endless details to lose yourself in, something new to explore with every glance. Ritchie's work appeals to all ages and he is enjoying a growing demand for his work. His work is exhibited worldwide and can be found in many private collections.

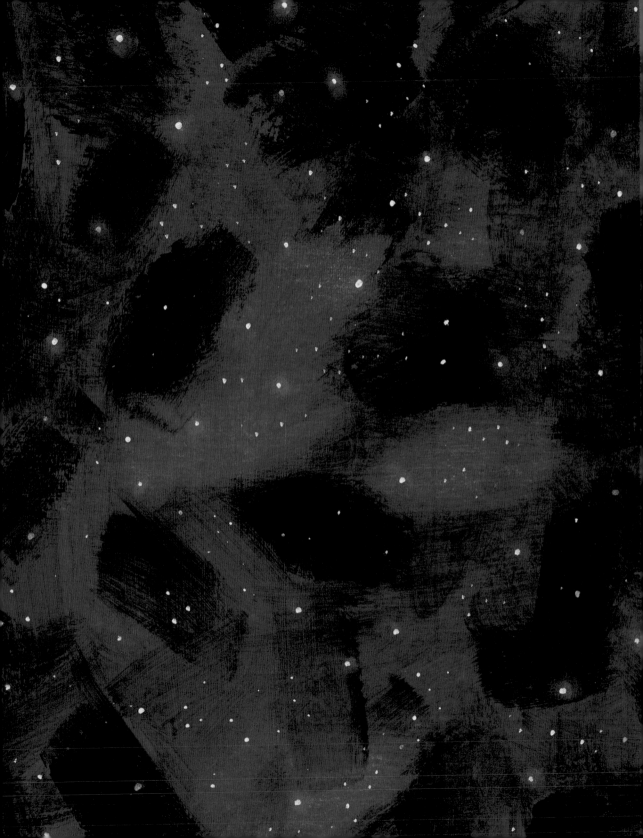